CU00916966

Euripides'

A NEW VERSION BY FRANK McGUINNESS

Euripides (c. 482–406 BC), dramatist of Ancient Greece, youngest of the three great tragic writers. Eighteen of some ninety plays attributed to him have survived, among them *Alcestis*, *Medea*, *Hippolytus*, *Electra*, *The Trojan Women* and *The Bacchae*. *Helen* was among the last of his plays, dating from 412 BC.

Frank McGuinness was born in Buncrana, Co. Donegal, and now lives in Dublin and lectures in English at University College Dublin. His plays include: *The Factory Girls* (Abbey Theatre, Dublin, 1982), *Baglady* (Abbey, 1985), *Observe the Sons of Ulster Marching Towards the Somme* (Abbey, 1985; Hampstead Theatre, London, 1986), *Innocence* (Gate Theatre, Dublin, 1986), *Carthaginians* (Abbey, 1988; Hampstead, 1989), *Mary and Lizzie* (RSC, 1989), *The Bread Man* (Gate, 1991), *Someone Who'll Watch Over Me* (Hampstead, West End and Broadway, 1992), *The Bird Sanctuary* (Abbey, 1994), *Mutabilitie* (NT, 1997), *Dolly West's Kitchen* (Abbey, 1999; Old Vic, 2000), *Gates of Gold* (Gate, 2002), *Speaking Like Magpies* (Swan, Stratford, 2005) and *There Came a Gypsy Riding* (Almeida, London, 2007). His widely performed versions include *Rosmersholm* (1987), *Yerma* (1987), *Peer Gynt* (1988), *Three Sisters* (1990), *The Threepenny Opera* (1991), *Hedda Gabler* (1994), *Uncle Vanya* (1995), *A Doll's House* (1997), *The Caucasian Chalk Circle* (1997), *Electra* (1998), *The Storm* (1998), *Miss Julie* (2000), *Hecuba* (2004), *Phaedra* (2006), *The Lady from the Sea* (2008) and *Oedipus* (2008).

also by Frank McGuinness

GATES OF GOLD
DOLLY WEST'S KITCHEN
MARY AND LIZZIE
SOMEONE WHO'LL WATCH OVER ME
MUTABILITIE
OBSERVE THE SONS OF ULSTER MARCHING TOWARDS THE SOMME
SPEAKING LIKE MAGPIES
THERE CAME A GYPSY RIDING

FRANK McGUINNESS PLAYS ONE
(*The Factory Girls,*
Observe the Sons of Ulster Marching Towards the Somme,
Innocence, Carthaginians, Baglady)

FRANK McGUINNESS PLAYS TWO
(*Mary and Lizzie, Someone Who'll Watch Over Me,*
Dolly West's Kitchen, The Bird Sanctuary)

Translations
A DOLL'S HOUSE (Ibsen)
PEER GYNT (Ibsen)
ELECTRA (Sophocles)
OEDIPUS (Sophocles)
THE STORM (Ostrovsky)
HECUBA (Euripides)
MISS JULIE (Strindberg)
PHAEDRA (Racine)
THE LADY FROM THE SEA (Ibsen)

Screenplays
Brian Friel's DANCING AT LUGHNASA

THE DAZZLING DARK: NEW IRISH PLAYS
(edited by Frank McGuinness)

EURIPIDES

Helen

a new version by
Frank McGuinness

from a literal translation by
Fionnuala Murphy

faber and faber

First published in 2009
by Faber and Faber Limited
74–77 Great Russell Street, London WC1B 3DA

Typeset by Country Setting, Kingsdown, Kent CT14 8ES
Printed in England by CPI Bookmarque, Croydon, Surrey

A CIP record for this book
is available from the British Library

ISBN 978-0-571-25251-0

2 4 6 8 10 9 7 5 3 1

In memory of Stewart Parker

Helen, in this version by Frank McGuinness, was first performed at Shakespeare's Globe, Bankside, London, on 2 August 2009. The cast was as follows:

Helen Penny Downie
Theonoe Diveen Henry
Pollux James Lailey
Gatekeeper Penny Layden
Castor Fergal McElherron
Menelaus Paul McGann
Theoclymenes Rawiri Paratene
Servant Ian Redford
Messenger Ukweli Roach
Teucer Andrew Vincent
Chorus Holly Atkins, Philip Cumbus, Jack Farthing, Tom Stuart, Graham Vick
Singer William Purefoy

Musical Director Phil Hopkins
Musicians Irita Kutchmy, Dai Pritchard

Director Deborah Bruce
Designer Gideon Davey
Composer Claire van Kampen
Choreographer Siân Williams
Fight Director Kevin McCurdy
Movement Work Glynn MacDonald
Voice and Dialect Work Jan Haydn Rowles

Characters

Helen
the stolen Queen of Sparta

Teucer
a wandering Greek soldier

Chorus
of Greek women

Menelaus
King of Sparta, abandoned husband to Helen

Gatekeeper
a woman in the service of Theoclymenes

Servant
an old sailor with Menelaus

Theonoe
Princess of Egypt, a prophetess

Theoclymenes
King of Egypt

Messenger
a man in the service of Theoclymenes

Castor
brother to Helen, now a god

Pollux
twin to Castor, now a god

HELEN

Setting

A graveyard in Egypt before the gates
of King Theoclymenes' royal palace

Time

Seventeen years after the Trojan War started,
when Helen was stolen from Sparta by Paris,
Prince of Troy, and taken from her husband,
Menelaus – apparently

Helen

My name is Helen – Helen of Egypt.
The river Nile is my neighbour here.
The King of this country – he's called Theoclymenes.
It's said he's devout – he adores the gods.
His sister, everyone's dote since she was a baby,
She's called Theonoe because she thinks like a god,
Knowing what is past or passing or to come.

I myself hail from heavenly Sparta.
I have one father, he's called Tyndareus –
However, there's another story told.
Zeus did it with my darling mother,
He was in the shape of a swan that night.
It was myself who sprang from their loins,
Me, Helen, and mine has not been a happy lot.
I've been the victim of woman's vanity.
Three powerful ladies ventured to Mount Ida –
I'll name them, Hera, Athena, Aphrodite,
None of them happy to come second in a beauty
    contest.
Clever Aphrodite, she knew what was what.
She promised me as prize to Paris,
Prince of Troy, judge of who was loveliest.
My beauty would be his – beauty, bane of my life,
I begrudge to no one, man, woman or child.
Paris came to Sparta to steal me from my marriage.
Hera had other plans – she was a woman scorned.
She was not so keen on this alliance.
Fair to say she'd blow it out of the water.

3

The goddess gathered elements of air –
She made a likeness of me, living, breathing,
She gave this ghost of myself to Paris,
Paris, son of Priam, King of strong Troy.
The same boy thinks he had me – he hasn't.
I'm afraid there is no Helen of Troy.

Zeus is not one ever to be outdone.
He'd even more fish to fry for our kind.
He spread war between Greek and poor Trojan.
A mad throng of men overran Mother Earth.
What's wrong? Does she want rid of us all?
Greece is all agog – who's her big hero?
The big row brewing between us and them,
And yours truly, the most splendid of spoils,
Helen, the woman from God knows where,
Not me, not in Troy, never set foot in it.

For this I have to thank Hermes for hiding me.
I glided in a cloud through the echelons of air.
I like to think Zeus was looking out for us.
That's why I landed on Egyptian earth,
Saving my bed for Menelaus, my husband.
My darling boy, he's called up all our men,
They'll travel to the towers of Ilium,
And to what end? All to bring me home.
How many have drowned in the drains of Troy –
How many have died because of me?
I have endured insult and injury –
I am called whore – worst word in their stomachs.
I am death to Greeks fighting this great war.

How did I go on? Hermes told me how,
That divine messenger, he gave me hope.
I will live again in the land of Sparta,
My husband will know I didn't go to Troy,
But I've to keep one side of the bargain.

I must not cavort in another man's bed.
That's the deal, and here's the rub, I'm not safe.
The King of Egypt has taken a shine to me.
More than a shine – he wants to marry me.
He's like an animal wanting to be fed.
A decent man, his father protected me.
That's why I perch on his holy grave.
These people worship the dead more than life itself.
Stuck here, his son won't lay a finger on me.
Ravage me and he'll feel his father's wrath.
And I owe my husband the honour due to him.
I will lie down with no fancy man.
Let Greeks hurl what names they like against me.
I'll bring no shame upon my body here.

Teucer enters.

Teucer

What sight is this – the woman I hate most?
Is she who destroyed me and all the Greeks?
Your murderous face – spit image of Helen –
May you be hated for being like her.
I would take great pleasure in removing you,
But I'm on foreign soil, rotten daughter of Zeus.

Helen

Why turn from me?
Why blame me for that woman's misfortunes?

Teucer

My anger – I've made a mistake.
All Greece hates Helen.
Forgive my words.

Helen

Why are you here – who are you?

Teucer

One of the wandering Greeks, woman.

Helen
    That's why you hate Helen – no wonder.
    Whose son are you – where are you from?

Teucer
    Teucer, Telamon's son, born and bred Salamis.

Helen
    What takes you to the waters of the Nile?

Teucer
    On the run from my native land.

Helen
    That's why you're suffering – who drove you away?

Teucer
    The man most near me, Telamon, my father.

Helen
    Then something is truly wrong –

Teucer
    My brother died at Troy – that's what finished me.

Helen
    You didn't down him with your own sword?

Teucer
    He did that deed all by himself – he took his life.

Helen
    Was he crazed? Who in his right mind –?

Teucer
    You've heard of the great Achilles?

Helen
    Indeed I have –
    He once came wooing Helen, I'm told.

Teucer
He died and there were ructions –
Who would get his armour?

Helen
Your brother was not happy?

Teucer
Another took the armour –
My brother took his life.

Helen
That's what ails you, his affliction?

Teucer
Because I didn't die with him, yes.

Helen
So, stranger, you saw the towers of Troy?

Teucer
I helped leave it in rubble –
The same state as myself.

Helen
It's already eaten by fire?

Teucer
Not even its smell survives.

Helen
The Trojans are destroyed because of damned Helen.

Teucer
Greeks as well – we're all done great wrong.

Helen
Did you hang the whore of Sparta?

Teucer
Helen? Menelaus dragged her by the hair.

Helen
That's not just hearsay?
Did you see the poor bitch?

Teucer
Saw her as sure as I see you.

Helen
You're certain?

Teucer
My eyes saw her – I'm certain.

Helen
Maybe it was the gods fooling –

Teucer
Change the subject – no more about her.

Helen
Menelaus – has he reached home with his wife?

Teucer
Nowhere near Greece, let alone Sparta.

Helen
Hard words. Not a good sign –

Teucer
Word is he's disappeared with her good self.

Helen
Were you Greeks not all sailing in one direction?

Teucer
We started out the same –
A storm separated us.

Helen
On what part of the sea?

Teucer

Middle of the Aegean.

Helen

Who knows if Menelaus arrived anywhere?

Teucer

All Greece believes he's a goner.

Helen

And Helen's mother – any news?

Teucer

Leda – is that who you mean? She's dead as dust.

Helen

Did the dirty about Helen –

Teucer

Destroy her mother? So they say.
She found a noose for her long, lovely neck.

Helen

Her sons – are they alive? Castor –

Teucer

And Pollux? Dead, but not dead.
Two sides to that story.

Helen

What do people believe?

Teucer

They have turned into the shape of stars.
The two are now gods in the sky.

Helen

That is well spoken.

Teucer

That's just one story.

Helen

Tell me the other.

Teucer

Because of their sister, they breathed their last.
That was their sacrifice – enough sad stories.
I came here for one single reason –
To see Theonoe, the prophetess. Arrange that.
She'll tell me how to sail straight to Cyprus.
Apollo promised me that is where I will live.

Helen

Trust the Nile, stranger – it will lead you there.
It flows from Egypt all the way to Cyprus.
Quit this house at once before the King sees you.
He hunts with his hounds now for bloodied beasts –
But he'll rip to pieces any Greek he captures.
Don't ask why – it would do you no good. Leave.

Teucer

Sound advice, woman – the gods reward you.
No denying – you do look like Helen.
A world of difference between you two.
May she stew in the cesspit she deserves.
I hope she will never set eyes on home.
But you, may you find good fortune always.

Teucer exits.

Helen is alone.

Helen

What is the grieving for?
Why am I weeping in pain?
Who listens to my lament?

Virgin daughters of the earth,
Maidens breathed by the wind,
Sirens – sing with me.

Bear witness to wild mourning
With Libyan flute or lyre.
Shed tears that rhyme with mine.
Suffer with my suffering.

I call on Persephone – listen,
In the dark of your darkest chambers
To my cries for my lost husband,
Perished, unprotected, life without luck.

The Chorus enters.

Chorus

I was drying my robes,
Purple in dark and blue water.
I heard a cry of horror.
A lament, a woman singing.
Who is ravaged – who is mourning?
Is it you grieving?
Why weep – what is the pity?

Helen

Women of Greece, foreign ships slaved you.
You know the sea can bring sorrow.
It sent a sailor to me, a wanderer.
It fetched me word from home to flay my heart.
Troy has fallen – I am its ruination.
Mention Helen's name, your days are numbered.
I am cursed for the living and the dead.
My shame drove my mother to hang herself.
My husband now is married to the sea.
Castor and Pollux, my two brothers –
One twin is the other, vanished, vanished.
Their horses' backs are bare, they fight no more.

Chorus

Lady, I hear your litany of misery.
I link it to the wonder of your birth.
Zeus and your mother, the god showed himself –

He showered no mercy on you, Helen,
For Leda now is dead, cold in the earth,
Her boys are buried above in the sky.
Will you ever set foot or see home again?
Every word in every mouth whispers,
You will lie down in a barbaric bed.
Your man is no more, the sea bares his bone,
He will not walk back to his father's house.

Helen

I see a tree in the forest,
I see it fall to the earth.
The bark and green branches,
I curse them fashioned into
A ship loaded with tears,
Tears for Greece, tears for Troy,
Carrying the son of Priam,
So he could seize my beauty
And marry it to misery.

Aphrodite, she comes with him,
A murderous avenger,
Hell bent on harming Greece,
Making me a misfortune.
But there is another goddess,
Revered Hera, in the arms of Zeus.
To save me she sends Hermes.
Those are wings sewn on his shoes.
He carries me through the clouds,
I land here, I live and know
I am dirt incarnate,
I caused the Trojan war.

Chorus

Endure what life throws you.
Learn – it's the only way.
We all suffer –

Helen

Do you say suffer, woman?
I was hatched from an egg –
A right, rare yolk.
Somewhat uncommon in Greece, that,
And among the savages.
Yes, the gods favoured me –

From birth I've been blemished.
Why did Zeus conceive me?
Was it to be a clown?
My beauty is a mask
Hera beat into shape,
A mask that mocks me.
Would I were a statue,
Wiped off the face of Earth –
Ugly, to be demolished,
Leaving next to no trace
But the good deeds I did,
And the bad forgotten.

So, you say endure – suffer.
I would do so gladly,
If mine were one misfortune.
I would bear the gods' grudge,
But I am worn down,
Worn by the weight of many woes.

My name is black, though I'm blameless.
Innocent, I stand convicted –
Worst of all judgements.
The gods remove me from home,
I am stranded among barbarians.
None of my own are near me.
A free woman, I'm slaved here
In this country of slaves.
My hope against hope – my husband –

13

He is hope abandoned.
He will not come and save me.
Menelaus is dead.
I am my mother's murder.
Too harsh, I hear you say?
Such harshness is my lot.
My daughter, light of my life,
She'll turn grey, she'll wither
Into a dry old maid.
My brothers have left the Earth.
What I have is less than nothing.
I am as well off dead –
I am more dead than living.
Do you know what's worse to bear?
Say I did reach the shores of home –
They'd bar the doors against me.
Helen of Troy, she is no more –
She went down with Menelaus.
Yet if that man was still alive,
There are secret signs we share,
That's how we'd know each other.
Wishful thinking – that's not to be –
He will never get here safely.

So why do I go on living?
What has fate in store for me?
I marry a brute beast,
I banish all my troubles
And gorge at his groaning table?
Save me from that solution.
If a woman should hate her husband,
Then she will hate her own body.
Better off to die by hanging –
Found, feet dangling, by the servants.
Even they think that end demeaning.
There is a ritual they respect –

It's falling on the sword's tip.
Find the target stopping life and limb.
Could I rise to the occasion?
That's the pit I've sunk into.
Other women love their beauty,
Mine lacerates me.

Chorus
Helen, one thing to ask you –
You're sure he told the truth?
This stranger, the whole truth –

Helen
About my husband? He said he's perished –
Loud and clear –

Chorus
Many lies are loud and clear –

Helen
The truth can be as well –

Chorus
Why believe the bad and not the good?

Helen
Pure fear – that's why – pure terror.

Chorus
Do you have friends in that house?

Helen
All are, except the man who'd marry me.

Chorus
Go in there and ask his sister –
Ask Theonoe about Menelaus.
That lady knows all about the sea –
She is descended from water.
Ask does Menelaus see the sun still?

Let her give you an exact answer.
Then laugh or cry when you learn.
You can only lament knowing nothing.
I am happy to walk in there with you.
Women should always stand by women.

Helen

Those are wise words – I'll heed them.
Go in and face what has to be faced.
Come with me.

Chorus

Willingly.

Helen

What tears will I shed –

Chorus

Don't tempt fate, Helen –
You'll bring bad luck on yourself.
Be strong – be patient.
Pray for good fortune.

Helen

Who did they pray to,
The dying and the dead,
Mothers for their sons,
Sisters for their brothers?
I would shear my head,
Rip my face open,
Drown Greece with tears,
And flood wretched Troy.
I would bleed my nails,
I would stain my soft skin,
This is the face that torched
The citadels of Troy.
For this body, my body,
Her men and maidens burned.

The earth was quaking,
I gave birth to tears and blood.
Pray for good fortune?
No, pray for mercy.

Helen exits with the Chorus.

Menelaus enters.

Menelaus
I date my bad luck from the day I was born.
No, I'll go further back.
Better my father had cursed his father,
He brought him into this hard world.
Then we would not exist, that mighty pair,
Menelaus myself and Agamemnon.
Though I'm not one to boast, we were the boys –
We led the biggest army ever to Troy,
Over the sea bleeding, black with oars.
I'm no tyrant – no man was forced to join.
Young men fell over themselves to enlist.
I let them for I was quick to lead them.
I know how many won't be coming back.
We bring home only the names of the dead.
I have been lost since in the lonely water,
Wandering since I laid waste to Troy.
All I want, all I crave is home – go home.
But the gods have decided to deny me.
I am not worth granting that gift.
I'm being thrown from pillar to post –
One hellhole after another hellhole,
All the landing spots of Libya.
When I get sight or sound of my country,
The winds turn their sour breath against me.
It drives me further from my fatherland.

The ship is now wrecked, and my comrades lost.
I'm cast aside onto this foreign shore.

All that's left of the vessel is the keel,
So lovely once, now smashed against the rocks.
By some stroke of luck, I clung on to it –
I was saved, Helen as well – she is here.
I dragged her screaming from her den in Troy.

I do not know this place or its people.
Don't ask why I parade in filthy rags –
I cannot face a crowd questioning me.
When a big man hits the skids, he sinks far –
He's just not used to being down and out.
It's simple why – beggars can't be choosers.
I've no sustenance, nor stitch on my back.
All I've on me I ransacked from the wreck.
The sea has dined on my dainty garments.
The water's fleeced me of my finery.
The woman who began all my bothers –
Helen is hidden deep inside a cave.
My soldiers guard her, and they are well warned.

That's why I'm here, sniffing food for my men.
I spotted the walls surrounding this house –
The magnificent gates of a mighty man.
I'll risk my luck with the rich and lazy.
They might shell out something for my sailors.
Forget those without a pot to piss in –
Even if they wanted, they've nothing to give –
I wonder who it is minds the gates?
I need to share my troubles. Come out here.
Come out from the house – are you there? Come out.

The Gatekeeper, a woman, enters.

Gatekeeper
What's the racket? Away from here, hop it.
Who are you to bother your betters?
You're Greek – I can tell by the cut of you.
We're not so keen on your kind. We'll skin you.

Menelaus

Madam, keep a civil tongue, please.
There's no need to be abusive.

Gatekeeper

You look like a Greek, you smell like a Greek,
You quack like a Greek, I'd say you're a Greek.
I've a punishing entry policy.
No dogs, no Greeks – fuck off, foreign bastard.

Menelaus

Go in and announce these words to your master –
I am a shipwrecked sailor and the law,
It demands you protect –

Gatekeeper

The law might – we don't – pester someone else.

Menelaus

Do as I bid you – I'll go in myself.

Gatekeeper

You're pushing it, pal – get a move on.
Your arse might soon be skimming the road.

Menelaus

I have men at my beck and call, famous –

Gatekeeper

May I just observe, you and what army?
It's done a runner, you're on your ownio.

Menelaus

God, look at what I suffer – what I've lost.

Gatekeeper

Why the tears – why wet eyes – why pity you?

Menelaus

Fortune once smiled sweetly on me and mine.

Gatekeeper

Good – let them cry at your sob story.

Menelaus

Whose house is this – what country?

Gatekeeper

Egypt – that's where you are.

Menelaus

I have sailed to unfortunate Egypt –

Gatekeeper

I'll have you know the Nile is world-renowned.
Why unfortunate – why blame the poor river?

Menelaus

I don't – I blame my fate.

Gatekeeper

Put a tune to that, whistle it, mister –
We could all join in with the chorus.

Menelaus

Who rules this land? Is he in the house –?

Gatekeeper

He is not, and you should be laughing, boy.
He suffers from a strange allergy.
He sees your like, they sicken his stomach.

Menelaus

Why does he hate –?

Gatekeeper

Blow-ins? Herself, Helen – the swan's babby.
Do you not know she's nested in this house?

Menelaus

What do you mean?

Gatekeeper
Helen – Leda's youngster – she's inside here.

Menelaus
Where did she come from?

Gatekeeper
Sparta – where else?

Menelaus
When did she come here?

Gatekeeper
Just before the troubles began in Troy.
Look, slip away from this place, stranger.
Things are not well at home – not well at all.
This is not the best time to come calling.
The big man's upset. You won't save your skin here.
If you're caught, wave your windpipe goodbye.
Death is looking you in the face – depart.
That's my advice – my bark is worse than my bite.
When it comes to Greeks, I've had my moments.

The Gatekeeper exits.

Menelaus
She says this Helen is the child of Zeus.
There's only one Zeus, only one Sparta.
Could it be there is more than one Helen?
I have no idea what this all means,
But I do know I'll have my belly filled,
When they hear I lit the fire that torched Troy.
Men marvel at the name of Menelaus.
I'd better wait for the lord and master.
If he's out for blood, I'll hide who I am –
I can sneak back to the wreck of my ship.
If he's kindly, I'll beg him – feed the needy.
This is what I hate most, I am a king,

But I'm on my knees scraping and scrounging.
The old saying's true – want's the worst ally.

The Chorus enters.

Chorus
The maiden sang
Her prophecy.
The earth's black clay
Has not been flung
On Menelaus.

He's escaped darkness.
Where does he chart
The breaking wave
With broken oar?
The harbour
That is never home?
He'd rest his bones
And kiss his grave
Were it in Sparta.

Helen enters.

Helen
Theonoe's words are welcome –
My husband is alive,
Tempest-tossed upon the sea.
When he returns,
His suffering ended,
He will be well travelled.
One thing she did not reveal –
Should he get here, will he be safe?
Happy to learn he was alive,
I daren't ask out straight.
She says he's very near,
Shipwrecked with some of our own.
When will you come for me?
I'm worn out waiting for you.

She sees Menelaus.

Who is that savage creature?
Is he out to rough me up?
Is he in the King's pay?
Get away from here.
Touch me and I'll kick like a horse,
I'll roar like a lunatic.

Menelaus

Stop – you're running away – stop –
Why flee from me? I see you – I panic –

Helen

Women, be my witness.
This man wrongs me.
He wants to trap me.
Haul me to the King.
I want no art nor part –
I don't want this marriage.
I want away.

Menelaus

I am not a thief –
I am not a bad man.

Helen

Look at the shape of you –
You're not fit for company –
Your clothes –

Menelaus

Stop being afraid, stand still.
What do I see in you, woman?

The two speak together.

Together

Who are you?

Menelaus
Menelaus.

Helen
Helen.

Menelaus
Ten years at war, seven years wandering –

Helen
That's how long I've waited –

The two speak again together.

Together
Who are you?
Is it you?

Helen
Are you a gift of God –
Or are you just one of my own?

Menelaus
Are you from this place?
Are you a Greek woman?

Helen
A Greek woman.
I want to learn about you as well.

Menelaus
You are the image of Helen.

Helen
And you of Menelaus.

Menelaus
You have recognised the saddest of men.

Helen
Your wife's opening her arms –
Why aren't you running into them?

Menelaus
Don't touch these rags –
What kind of wife would –?

Helen
I am the wife my father gave to you.

Menelaus
Let me believe this magic –
What are you, woman?

Helen
I am not the ghost who haunts your nights.

Menelaus
I am not a husband who has two wives.

Helen
What other wife can claim you?

Menelaus
The one I brought from Troy.

Helen
You have no wife but myself.
Look at me – you need more proof?
Will you not believe your eyes?
I did not go to Troy.

Menelaus
Who did, then?

Helen
A dream – an illusion that came to life.

Menelaus
Who can create a living illusion?

Helen
The gods can – out of air.

Menelaus
Which god?

Helen
Hera – she made a copy of me,
Paris would not win me.

Menelaus
Were you in Egypt –?
Were you in Troy –?
At one and the same time?

Helen
My name was, but I was not –
I remained myself.

Menelaus
Let go of me, woman –
I come here weighed down enough –

Helen
Are you going to leave me in this place?
Will you scarper off with a shadow?

Menelaus
I wish you all the best –
You do have the look of Helen.

Helen
Husband, I found you, but you fail me.
You do not trust –

Menelaus
These are my scars from Troy.
I trust them, not you.

Helen
What woman is worse off than this one?
Those I love most leave me.
I will not see Greece nor home again.

A Servant of Menelaus enters.

Servant
Menelaus, at long last I've found you –
I've searched every corner of this kip.

Menelaus
Are the savages attacking us?

Servant
A miracle has happened –
More than a miracle.

Menelaus
That's why you are in such a state –
You can barely breathe.

Servant
All you've suffered's been in vain.

Menelaus
That's a well-worn lament –
What's the new one?

Servant
Your wife has vanished –
Disappeared into the air.
We hid her in the cave,
But now heaven hides her.
She said these words to us:
'Poor men of Troy, all you Greeks,
Did you die for my sake,
Did you perish in the great war?
Hera's pulled a fast one –
Paris thought he had Helen.
He was quite mistaken.
I kept the game going,
Yes, I did my bit,
But heaven is my father,

He wants me to go home.
The worst word has been hurled
At Leda's sad daughter,
But Helen was beyond reproach.'

The Servant notices Helen.

So you've landed here, great lady –
Allow me to salute you.
I've declared you could spout wings,
Ascend to the highest heavens.
You laugh at us again –
I can no longer allow that.
Your husband and his men, at Troy,
You put us through hell and high water.

Menelaus

Leave her be – it's all as she's said.
She spoke the absolute truth.
This is the day I've longed for –
I take my wife in my two arms.

Helen

Look, friends, my happiness – my husband.
I throw myself at him.
He is the sun shining in my eyes.

Menelaus

My tongue is tied –
Words on the leash.
Where do I begin?

Helen

The hair stands on my head,
My eyes dripping with tears.

Menelaus

My hands cannot leave your flesh.
So much pleasure I fear it.

Helen

The sight I love most – my husband.

Menelaus

Daughter of Zeus and Leda,
My wife, I do not complain.

Helen

My friends, I do not lament –
I've waited, year after year –
Now I have him come from Troy.

Menelaus

At long last God's smiled on me –
I'm crying with joy.
These tears are gratitude, not grief.

Helen

Do I really hold you to me?

Menelaus

Sure as I am holding you –
Answer this for me, in God's name –
Who spirited you away?

Helen

Hera – up to her pure badness.

Menelaus

Why would she afflict us?

Helen

To spite Paris – to spite Aphrodite.
She it was brought me to Egypt.
Now we stand together desolate.
The golden army of Greece is gone.

Menelaus

Paris ransacked my home top to bottom.

Helen

I didn't leave your marriage bed –
I didn't shame you –

Menelaus

Was it all illusion?

Servant

Menelaus, you're a changed man – why?
Let me in on –

Menelaus

You're in the right there, old boy.
You should be party to all of this.
Here is a happy turn of events –

Servant

This madam – is she not the cause –
The source of all our suffering in Troy?

Menelaus

The gods made a mockery of us.
She was not there. She was never there.

Servant

The war was for nothing?
We endured all we endured –
We fought for something that never was?
You tell me now, this one, this woman –
She is really your wife?

Menelaus

She really is.

Servant

The gods are changeable as a child's arse.
Who knows if they work for or against you?
A man suffers, they smile, then he prospers.
They change their tune, poor bugger dies roaring.
Security – you can forget that foolishness.

You two have not travelled an easy journey.
This woman's had to hear the bitterest words,
And himself's had to tear down all-comers.
He's got nothing till now for all his pains.
Let him stand back and enjoy his good luck.

You didn't shame your father or brothers.
You're innocent of all accusation.
I can recall the day of your wedding.
I remember carrying lighted torches,
Racing alongside your hoard of horses,
You the bride in your chariot with this man.
Stand together through thick as well as thin,
Always been my motto – servants should serve.
I've brains in my head as much as the rest.
I'm next to nothing but I'll think for myself.
Better that than stinking of slavery.

Menelaus

You've been through the wars for my sake, old man.
Go and share my good news with the friends waiting.
Tell them what's the present state of affairs.
Expect trouble for myself and this woman.
Be ready in case we can run out of here.
If we give the barbarians the slip,
Then we'll be out of this trap together.

Servant

I'll do as you demand, my lord Menelaus.
Before I go, I'll tell you something for nothing.
Prophecy's a mug's game – a complete con.
How can a body read flames in the fire?
What can you learn from the squawking of birds?
Our feathered friends can reveal our future?
How in hell do they? It's all utter tosh.
We had a fair few could see secret signs –
The Trojans too, some of them had the gift.

They witnessed only what we witnessed.
Give the boys who read futures a far berth.
All they deliver is easy dreams.
Do damn all but burn bits of sacrifice.
That's how you'll line those parasites' pockets.
We all saw a city ripped asunder,
Men breathing their last – for the sake of what?
An illusion, a dream – nothing, nothing.
We fought the Trojan War over nothing.

The Servant exits.

Chorus

Respect the gods –
Keep in with the gods –
They'll save you from false prophets.

Helen

Menelaus, you must leave with him.
Flee from here.
The man who owns this house will kill you.

Menelaus

Why pay me such special attention?

Helen

You know, you might embarrass him –
At his wedding – to me – your wife.

Menelaus

Did you stretch yourself out beside him?

Helen

I slept alone – waiting for you to show.

Menelaus

You say I can't bring you home –

Helen

A big sword is in the way, not my bed.
Get away –

Menelaus
And abandon you?

Helen
Do you imagine you can kill the King?

Menelaus
For you, I burned Troy to the ground.

Helen
Good for you, but now it's time to think.

Menelaus
So I'm to run like a woman?

Helen
We're in a serious fix.

Menelaus
Better to go down fighting –

Helen
Think – think quick –

Menelaus
Than to die like a dog.

Helen
One way only we can be saved.
Say the King doesn't know you've arrived –

Menelaus
How could he know – who'll tell him?

Helen
His sister, Theonoe – a prophet –
She's inside the house.
She has the power of a god.
That woman knows all things.
She'll tell her brother you're here.

Menelaus
I'm a dead man – I can't get away –

Helen
We might sway her – beg her –

Menelaus
Do what? What hope –?

Helen
Beg her say nothing about you.

Menelaus
Then we can hot-foot it?

Helen
Her with us, easy.
Without her, impossible.

Menelaus
I'll leave that up to you.
This is stuff for the ladies.

Helen
I'll do what needs doing.

Menelaus
If she doesn't buy it?

Helen
You're for the chop – I'm for the altar.

Menelaus
Will they really have to drag you?
Is that what you do want?
Treacherous bitch –

Helen
I swear one sacred vow to you –

Menelaus
You'd die before you'd stain your wedding sheets?

Helen

On the same sword as you die.
I lie next to my husband only.

Menelaus

Touch my right hand.

Helen

I touch it.
If you die, I leave the light of day.

Menelaus

If I lose you, I end my life.

Helen

How do we die and gain glory?

Menelaus

I'll kill you where we stand – then kill myself.
First, I'll take on all-comers against us.
Line them up, men who boast they're brave enough.
No shame in store for the man who tamed Troy.
I defy Greece – throw nothing in my face.
I did all I did to win back my wife.
I sent cold Achilles' corpse to his mother.
I saw Nestor left without son or heir.
It's right I do battle for my wife's sake.
Gods cast cowards aside to rot on rocks.

There is the sound of bolts being drawn.

Helen

Menelaus, the house is resounding –
The door bolts are loosened – we are done for.
Theonoe comes from the palace – flee.
No, why should you? She knows where you are.
Misfortune, you've beaten me black and blue.
You got away, husband, from fallen Troy –
Now you have to face whatever's in store.

Theonoe enters with Servants carrying fire.

Theonoe
Carry that torch before me.
Perform the holy ritual –
Purify the divine air.
I wish to breathe the air of heaven.

Look to the path before me,
Cleanse it with fire so I may pass –
Observe devotion to the gods,
Bring flames back to my hearth.

The ritual of purification is now complete.

Do you believe me, Helen?
Are my prophecies correct?
Has Menelaus arrived?
Has he lost his ships?
Has he lost your shadow?

She turns to Menelaus.

You have defied all's been done against you.
You don't know will you stay here or see home?
Zeus has gathered the great gods together.
You are their business – there's bother stirring.
Hera once would harm you – now she's changed
    her tune.
She wants you and Helen safe back in Sparta.
She wants Greece to know Aphrodite cheats.
The marriage made with Paris was a sham.
Her beauty won the prize – no, she bought it,
It's payback time – she'll wreck your return.
I must decide how this will be resolved.
Do I tell you are here and destroy you?
That is what a certain goddess is demanding.
What should I do – side instead with Hera?

Do I save your life and hide all I know –
My brother insists I inform on spies.
Dangerous, dangerous, too dangerous –
Let my brother know this man has arrived.

Helen kneels.

Helen
I beg for my life and for my man's life.
For seventeen years I've barely held him,
Now am I going to see him slaughtered?
I pray – give my loved husband back to me.
Save him – don't stain your soul for your brother.
His gratitude would be wrong and wicked.
He loves what God hates, that is violence.
Have nothing to do with his selfishness.
Heaven is made for each and every one of us,
So is this Earth – take what's yours and no more.
My husband wants his wife, he wants me back.
If he's put to the sword, can he do that?
Follow God's will in this – your father would.
For this he sheltered me in safe Egypt.
Don't begrudge what belongs to your neighbour.
Your sacred father towers above you.
He would condemn your brother's boorishness.
Pervert your father's justice – pervert yourself.
You, a prophet, stand in awe of the gods.
You know what's past, what's passing and to come.
But do you know what is right and lawful?

Not a living soul does not hate Helen.
Greece believes I did the dirty on him –
I swanned off to the filthy nest of Paris.
I plied my trade round the towers of Troy.
Let me set foot back again in Sparta.
Let people see the gods were playing games.
I am not a traitor to my own kind.

I will be an honest woman once more,
Honoured, happy to betroth my daughter.
I'll leave this bitter beggar's life behind.
In my own home I'll enjoy what's mine.

Had this man perished burning on the pyre,
I would have drowned him with my distant tears
Though I was far away from him I love.
Now he is beside me – he is alive –
Am I going to be deprived of him?
Lady, I entreat you, grant this favour,
Show you are your just father's just daughter.
Match goodness with goodness like that great man –
The precious gift child can give to parent.

Chorus

Your words would move a stone to soften –
Woman, you'd turn that same stone to pity.
How will Menelaus plead for his life?

Menelaus

I won't lower myself – fall at your feet –
I won't let my eyes shed a single tear.
That would be the carry-on of a coward.
I won't make Troy blush that I butchered her.
Men should weep in bad times – powerful men –
They say that's sure sign of nobility.
Not by my reckoning – give me courage.
All I ask you is save a stranger's life –
A stranger seeking to win back his wife.
Give her to me, let us live together.
Deny me, I'll add that to my misfortunes –
You'll prove yourself a dishonest woman.

I fall on your father's tomb, I say this:
Good man in the cold grave, return my wife.
Zeus sent her here to you for safe keeping.
You are dead now, you cannot keep your word –

You, revered and renowned, I call on you –
I call on you below, ask your daughter,
Is she woman enough to be your blood
And act fairly – all is in her hands.

Now I pray to Hades, god of the dead –
My sword stuffed your belly full of dead men
For the sake of this woman, kind Helen.
You've had your good gettings – I want them back,
Or make that daughter honour her father –
Give me what I want, I ask for my wife.
Remove my lady from me, I will be obliged
To engage in fiercest fisticuffs,
If we care to step out and settle this,
One boot in the balls against the other.
I will slice your brother in bits, madam.
Fight to the death – the stark, simple story.
Should he starve us as we sit at the tomb,
Two supplicants, I have my mind made up –
I kill Helen, then kill myself.
Streams of blood are the stains we leave behind,
A scream of pain to turn you into stone,
Hard heart against us, against your father.
Your brother will not marry this woman.
If home is the hard pit of Earth, so be it –
We go home – better death than desertion.
Why do I bother pleading a man's cause?
Cry like a woman, I'd win sympathy.
Are we no more than rats to be removed?
Have us two put down, if you think that's just.
No, stop – be swayed – give me my gentle wife.

Chorus
Everything lies with you, my lady.
You're the one must judge.
And you have to please everybody.

Theonoe

 It's in my nature to do the right thing.
 My father's good name is holy to me.
 I'll not allow my brother to tarnish it.
 My ancestors bred justice in my bones.
 Menelaus, they are what will guide me.
 Since Hera smiles on you, she gets my vote.
 I am a virgin no man violates –
 Aphrodite can be angry as she likes,
 I am not scared of her shenanigans.

 I answer you then at my father's tomb,
 It is wrong not to give you back your wife.
 Had my father lived, he would have done so –
 Handed you to her, handed her to you.
 He saved her from death, I save you for life.
 I have no say in my brother's badness.
 It's a good thing I stop him in his tracks.
 All is settled, I stand back in silence.
 Now you have to find your way out of here.
 Pray to the gods, pray to Aphrodite –
 Beg her allow you return to Sparta.
 Beg Hera to save you and your husband,
 Beg her stay true to her solemn promise.
 I turn to my dead father in his grave –
 You will never be branded a bad man,
 Not while there is breath left in my body.

 Theonoe exits into the palace.

Chorus

 The good won't go under.
 Honest men don't fear heaven.

Helen

 Menelaus, this woman saves us.
 We have to escape together.
 We two need to think as one.

Menelaus

You must know his servants well –
You've slept for years under his roof.

Helen

What does that mean?
Is it help or hindrance?
What's stirring in your head?

Menelaus

He has horsemen – they have chariots –
Could you persuade them to part with one?

Helen

To what use – how do we escape?
This country is strange – what's the way out?
How do we find the right road?

Menelaus

Say I hide in the palace – I knife the King –

Helen

His sister sees all – she will tell –

Menelaus

We're short of a ship to sail away –
The sea has the one we did have.

Helen

Listen – do you trust a woman's wit?
You're not a dead man –
Will you be spoken of as such?

Menelaus

Can that be lucky? Who cares –
It might work – say I'm dead –

Helen

I'd have to mourn you – fool the King –
Cut my hair – loud lamenting –

Menelaus

He'll swallow that?

Helen

You're drowned – we know the niceties of death –
Certain decencies must be observed –
There has to be a burial at sea –
Even if we're short of a body.

Menelaus

So you can honour my corpse.
Say he does agree to that –
How can we get away? We have no ship.

Helen

Get him to give me a boat.
I drop my gifts into your grave –
Right there at the bottom of the sea.

Menelaus

Fine and dandy, I'm thinking –
But say he insists on dry land –

Helen

It is not done among the Greeks,
Being a mysterious shower,
To drown on dry land.

Menelaus

Right – right you be.
So, I stand with you on the same ship –
I send the spoils into the deep –

Helen

You have to be there, yes –
And your sailors who survive.

Menelaus

I seize the ship at anchor –
My men ready with their swords –

Helen

The winds let the sails race us home –
You are in complete control.

Menelaus

I am –
Wait, who got you word I drowned?

Helen

You did – who else?
You started out with Menelaus,
You saw him die – you were spared his sad fate.

Menelaus

These rags wrapped around me –
They're witness to the shipwreck.
What do I do – go in with you?
Or sit silent by the tomb?

Helen

This tomb and your own sword protect you.
Stay – I'll go in on my own to the house.
I'll trim my hair, throw on a few black robes –
I'll trickle blood down my cheek with my nails.
It will be tough – things could go either way.
For this I'm put to death or I save your life.

Hera who sweetens the soft bed of Zeus,
Embroidered with the silver stars of heaven,
Goddess, relieve two mortals' suffering.
And I ask Aphrodite, don't harm me.
Why do you take such delight in deceit?
Why are you hellbent on my destruction?
Why are you so hungry for human blood?
You drain our veins dry to cast your spells,
You cry with laughter at catastrophe,
Show some give and take – some sign of fairness –
Become the goddess we love to worship.
I'll leave it at that – let sleeping dogs lie.

Helen exits into the palace.

Chorus

I call on the sorrowful nightingale,
Perched in her leafy shelter, singing bird –
Weep for Helen, for Troy and its daughters,
Lamenting death brought by grey-waved waters,
Tearing hair from their head in golden shards,
Mourning lost warriors, lonely and pale.
Your winged father, Zeus, the exquisite,
Begot you, Helen, in your mother's womb.
Your birth was the death of that great city,
Its streets and towers are now opened tombs.
What was that fight for – illusion and dream?
Are gods like men – nothing is what it seems?
Sad nightingale, poor birds of the air,
Sing the damnation of all warmongers.

Theoclymenes enters from the hunt with Servants.

Theoclymenes

I salute the grave of my father.
Proteus, I buried you beside this house
So I could bless you as I come and go.
In homage to you, highest in heaven,
Your son Theoclymenes, bows down,
Exalted father, venerated on earth.
Slaves – get the dogs and nets inside now.

The Servants exit into the palace.

I'm too soft-hearted – a failing of mine.
I shy away from extreme punishments.
The death penalty deters nobody –
Criminals swarm like flies about shit.
Speaking of which – a Greek's been seen landing –
In the pure light of day slipped past the guards.
He must be a spy, or after Helen.
No more pussyfooting – that man will die.

44

He notices Helen is gone.

Am I too late – has this indeed happened?
Helen has flown from her perch at the tomb.
Has she been stolen away from the land?
Throw open every door – clear the stables –
Bring every chariot – stop her escaping –
Stop – I see she has not done a runner.
You – why have your swapped your white robes for
    black?
You've chopped your hair off your lovely head – why?
Why are you lamenting – is it bad dreams?
Some word from home has left you grief stricken?

Helen

All I have is gone – I'm done for, master.
My master, my lord, my new name's for you.

Theoclymenes

What is amiss – what misfortune –?

Helen

Menelaus – how can I say the sound?
Menelaus – Menelaus has died on me.

Theoclymenes

I wanted this, but I take no joy –
How do you know – did Theonoe tell?

Helen

She did – so did he – that man saw –

Theoclymenes

Who is he – where?

Helen

Him, trembling by the tomb.

Theoclymenes

His clothes stink to high heaven – ugly –

Helen

So would my husband's, I suppose.

Theoclymenes

What country is he from?

Helen

Greece.

Theoclymenes

How did he land here?

Helen

A sailor – shipwrecked with my husband.

Theoclymenes

What kind of death did Menelaus suffer?

Helen

A sad one in the sea's watery waves.

Theoclymenes

How did this fellow not die?

Helen

Fortune gives the nod to those with nothing.

Theoclymenes

Is anything left of the lost ship?

Helen

It sank to the bottom of the sea.
So did Menelaus, but that man's saved.
I know where he'd lie, had I my way.

Theoclymenes

How did he arrive on these shores?

Helen

Pure chance – a boat picked him up.

Theoclymenes
That thing sent instead of you to Troy –
What's become of that?

Helen
Melted into air – thin air.

Theoclymenes
Poor Priam – Troy fell in vain.

Helen
I shared my luck with the sons of Priam.

Theoclymenes
And he left your husband unburied?

Helen
Cold without clay – it's why I mourn him.

Theoclymenes
That's why you've cut your golden hair –

Helen
He is still dear to me as if he's here.

Theoclymenes
You have good reason to shed sore tears.
How do I know he tells the truth?

Helen
Does your sister believe lies?

Theoclymenes
She does not.

Helen
She believes him.

Theoclymenes
What will you do now? This tomb – still your haunt?

Helen
My husband is gone – I must honour him –
For in my mind he lives –

Theoclymenes
Why mock me – leave the dead to the dead.

Helen
A husband finds a home – a wife follows.

Theoclymenes
So you flee from me – that's how you're faithful?

Helen
I can take no more of this – no more –
The wedding – start preparing now.

Theoclymenes
A long time coming, those words –
But I'm content at last to hear them.

Helen
You know what has to be done.
Forget all that's gone before.

Theoclymenes
One favour deserves another – the deal?

Helen
A truce between us – it's time for peace.

Theoclymenes
Our quarrel is ended – let it vanish.

Helen kneels before Theoclymenes, grasping his knees in supplication.

Helen
I thrown myself to my knees – I beg you –

Theoclymenes
Why behave like this – what do you want?

Helen
  Bury my dead husband.

Theoclymenes
  A tomb for a body who is not there?
  Will you put his ghost in the earth?

Helen
  Greeks have a custom –
  Anyone who dies at sea –

Theoclymenes
  What's the done thing? You know how these things –

Helen
  Dress a mask of the man in fine garments –
  That's how we bury dead sailors.

Theoclymenes
  I know nothing of your ways.

Helen
  Throw into the sea all the dead will need.

Theoclymenes
  What do I need to provide?

Helen
  This man can tell you.

Theoclymenes
  Stranger, your news is welcome –

Menelaus
  Not to me, nor the man who's passed away.

Theoclymenes
  How do you bury those the sea's taken?

Menelaus
  Each one according to his wealth.

Theoclymenes
Take what you wish, for this woman's sake.

Menelaus
First we spill blood as sacrifice.

Theoclymenes
From which animal?

Menelaus
You choose – we need a perfect specimen.
A bed – a bier – with no body on it.

Theoclymenes
Consider it done – what else is needed?

Menelaus
Armour – forged, the best of bronze.
A mighty man with the spear – Menelaus.

Theoclymenes
Honour the dead Greek with all –

Menelaus
We need more – each fresh fruit the earth gives.

Theoclymenes
And deposit the lot in the sea?

Menelaus
We need a ship standing by – men who can row.

Theoclymenes
How far from the shore will it go?

Menelaus
The human eye will strain to see it.

Theoclymenes
Why do Greeks follow that custom?

Menelaus
Tides can't carry back what the dead defile.

Theoclymenes
A fast Phoenician ship –

Menelaus
Will do us proudly – it'd please Menelaus.

Theoclymenes
You won't need Helen to be there –

Menelaus
A mother's duty, a wife and children's –
Shed sore tears, and tear what's left of their hair.

Theoclymenes
This woman has to bury her husband –

Menelaus
Don't deprive the dead of their due –
There's no luck otherwise.

Theoclymenes
I'll encourage loyalty in a wife –
So let her go, that will pay off for me.
Go inside, take whatever the dead need.
Cover yourself, eat to your heart's content –
You now haven't the nails to scratch yourself,
Whatever helps you to get home, take it.
Poor Helen, no point crying your eyes out.
You're still hale and hearty, but Menelaus –
Well, he's met his fate – stop pining for him.
You cannot weep a dead man back to life.

Menelaus
You know what you have to do, good woman.
Your husband's in front of you, be happy.
Let the last fellow go, he is no more.

The best I can do is go back to Greece,
Put a stop to the slurs thrown against you.
I do warn you that depends on yourself –
Be the good wife you should be to your partner.

Helen

My husband will never find fault with me.
All who stand in this place, be my witness.
Poor man, go inside, take a bath and change.
Rely on me – the more I do for you,
The more you serve my beloved Menelaus.
I will do all I can to assist you.

*Helen and Menelaus, with Theoclymenes at their
head, exit into the palace.*

Chorus

I call the Mother of Earth, Demeter,
To leave the rivers and roaring seas
Bereft of every living creature.
I see that goddess take a wild beast's shape
Hearing her daughter's unending plea –
'Avenge me, Mother, for my savage rape.'

Denying humankind its sustenance,
She leaves them grassless – the fields once fertile –
The herds are starving and in hunger's dance,
The gods themselves hear their bellies rumbling.
She makes of heaven a hideous hell
Commanding flesh and fish and fowl take wing.

Pray to Demeter to spare the rod,
Wear garlands of ivy and pour her wine –
Magnificent Helen, daughter of God,
Give to the great mother the moon and sun.

Helen enters from the palace.

Helen

It's all working out well for us inside –
Theonoe is helping our plan to hatch.
She says nothing about seeing Menelaus.
My husband stumbled on a bit of luck –
The armour he was to throw in the sea,
He can carry the spear in his right hand
And put his strong arm through the shield's strap.
He pretends to pay homage to the dead.
You might say he is well geared for battle,
Ready to beat the barbarians to pulp.
I've decked him out well – his clothes a credit –
Soaked his skin in a bath – I love his smell –
First time in ages fresh water has touched him.
I have to hold my tongue – keep up this show.
That man thinks we'll tie the knot together,
Him, coming from the house – you say nothing –
Stay on my side. If we can save ourselves,
One day we might be able to save you.

Theoclymenes enters from the palace with Servants
and Menelaus in fine clothes and armour.

Theoclymenes

Bring out the offerings for burial.
Proceed, my slaves – carry them to the sea.
Helen, do as I ask you and stay here –
I think your late husband possesses you.
You'll throw yourself into the swelling sea.
There seems no end to your grieving for him.

Helen

My dear husband-to-be, I know what to do.
Honour the partner I shared my bed with.
To that dead man I first gave my body –
I swear I would die out of love for him,
But how could that aid and abet his soul?

53

Let me go and mourn his memory.
I pray the gods give you all you deserve –
The King desires a wife – grant his desire –
You've been so sweet to me and Menelaus.
Things look decidedly on the bright side.
Show us a ship to cart these offerings,
I'll feel then the full weight of your kindness.

Theoclymenes
It will have fifty oars – rowers as well –

Helen
The man in charge of the funeral cortège –
He should be captain as well.

Theoclymenes
My sailors will obey him.

Helen
They must understand you clearly –
Repeat that order.

Theoclymenes
Till I'm blue in the face – if that please you.

Helen
May it please us both if all goes to plan.

Theoclymenes
Your tears – I worry – you might melt away.

Helen
Tears of gratitude you'll savour this day.

Theoclymenes
I dislike daytime – love the hour of night.

Helen
Who knows our day and hour – this world, the next –

Theoclymenes
   In me you'll have a husband to match Menelaus.

Helen
   Quite without fault – good fortune, smile on me.

Theoclymenes
   All down to you – provided you please me.

Helen
   No one need teach me how to love my friends.

Theoclymenes
   I have an idea –
   Should I go on board with you?
   Give you a hand –?

Helen
   Be my slave before your slaves?
   My lord, I don't think so – no, no, master.

Theoclymenes
   I'll leave you to your Grecian devices.
   Tell my people, prepare for my nuptials.
   The country must convulse with happiness.
   I marry Helen – singing everywhere.
   Laughter all round – let each man envy me.
   Stranger, give these offerings to the sea.
   Bring Helen back to our wedding breakfast.
   You can feast with us and make up your mind –
   Will you head off home or stay here and thrive?

   Theoclymenes exits into the palace.

Menelaus
   Our father Zeus, wisest of gods, protect us.
   Speed our journey through this roughest sea.
   Should your finger touch us then we are safe.
   Father, I've endured hardship after hardship.

The gods heard me curse the lot of them loud,
But I should not be punished forever.
Let me hold my head high once more – grant that,
I'll be at peace – a fortunate being.

Chorus
I call to mind a sea fleet as the winds,
A Phoenician frigate and its oars.
Dolphins speed the ship through tormented waves
That carry Helen home to kith and kin.
Let her sacrifice sacred blood and swear
She will give her daughter to men and love,
As Apollo did with his gorgeous lad
Beautiful Hyacinth, cold in the clay,
His soul a white bird guiding the big mast,
Bearing man and wife to their native land.
The waters speak – we end your toil, they say,
Poor seafarers, your wanderings have passed.
I call to mind a sea free as the wind.
I call to mind my Greece, my kith, my kin.

*A Messenger enters just as Theoclymenes comes out
of the palace.*

Messenger
The King – fetch out our King.

Theoclymenes
What is it?

Messenger
Helen is gone – Menelaus stole her.
He came himself to proclaim his death.

Theoclymenes
Your story beggars belief –
What ship carried them?

56

Messenger
The one you gave that stranger.
We reached it and set to work.
Greeks dressed in dirt approached –
Handsome, shipwrecked men.
Their boss spotted them and spoke,
Pity in his voice.

'Poor travellers, are you lost at sea?
Board here to bury Menelaus.
His weeping wife welcomes you –
She gives his ghost to a watery grave.'

Their tears mocked us.
We smelt a rat.
We whispered,
'It's getting crowded.'
But we said nothing,
Following orders.
The stranger spoke,
And we obeyed.
He was in charge –
That was your command,
But ill was in the air.

Then the bull would not budge,
His horns sharp as scythes,
No man could move him,
Till Helen's husband spoke.

'Brave boys of Greece, you put paid to Troy's pride.
Haul that brute on your shoulders like good men.
He's the sacrifice for our dead soldier.'

The sword raised in one hand,
Menelaus stroked his horse,
Eased it up the vessel.
Helen climbed on board –

A fine pair of ankles –
Sat next to the dead hero.
The rest crammed inside,
Spears hidden in their rags.
And the ship sailed on,
Leaving shore and land behind.

The bull bellowed.
Its throat was slit.
No mention of the dead –
Just prayers to Poseidon,
The guardians of the sea,
'Carry us home safely.'
Blood spouted from the beast –
Good sign for the stranger.
The bull now done and dusted,
Menelaus, he declared –
'Fine men of Greece, slaughter these savages,
What stops you hurling them into the tide?'

We were no pushover.
Swords stuck in our fists.
Grabbed the oars, smashed their brains out –
One side against the other.
Dainty Helen did her bit.
She was roaring from the rear –

'Where's the mettle you showed at Troy?
I want to see you squash this scum.
Lash in with no mercy – lash – lash –'

Men fell in the mayhem.
Some struggled to their feet.
Most were dead as dust.
Fair to say of Menelaus,
He has a nose for a fight,
Smelling out who needs a hand,
Parading in his armour,

58

Instantly on the spot,
His sword was the fear of God
He put into the lot of us.
We abandoned the oars,
Dropped like stones from the ship.
They steered straight to Greece,
They raised the masts.
The breeze blessed them on their way.

They are gone from the land.
I slid down the anchor.
That's what saved me.
I'd given up hope –
I saw a fishing boat,
It picked me from the sea.
I reached land to report this –
Learn one thing from this life,
Trust nobody, my lord.

Chorus

He's pulled the wool over our eyes,
Menelaus – he's done the same over yours –
Who could credit it, my lord and master?

Theoclymenes

The bride has bolted.
A woman's trick trumped me.
There'll be no back answers –
I cannot catch the ship.
But I'll have my revenge.
Sister, you stab me in the back –
You saw Menelaus.
Damn your dazzling visions.
You'll blind no more men.

Theoclymenes starts to go in.

The Gatekeeper stops him.

59

Gatekeeper
Where are you going – to commit murder?

Theoclymenes
I'll dish out rough justice – out of my way.

Gatekeeper
I will not let you go off, you –

Theoclymenes
You boss your master?
Woman, you're a slave –

Gatekeeper
And the slave's thinking straight –

Theoclymenes
I know what I have to do –

Gatekeeper
Over my dead body –

Theoclymenes
Kill my traitor sister –

Gatekeeper
She is the best of women –

Theoclymenes
Who betrayed me –

Gatekeeper
And she was right –

Theoclymenes
Robbing my bride to give another man –

Gatekeeper
A man who's more entitled –

Theoclymenes
Entitled to what is mine.

Gatekeeper
Menelaus is her man – her father gave her to him.

Theoclymenes
Fate gave her to me –

Gatekeeper
And fate's taken her from you.

Theoclymenes
Do you dare judge me?

Gatekeeper
I dare, for I talk sense – you don't, my lord.

Theoclymenes
You'd like to bathe in your own blood?

Gatekeeper
Send me to hell's gates –
Don't kill your sister.
I'll not let you.
Put me in her place.
The slave commands you –
Do what she bids.
Woman and all as I am,
I can die if I so choose –
A better man than you.

The Dioscuri appear from above.

They are twins, Castor and Pollux, divine brothers to Helen.

Castor
We are the Dioscuri.
Zeus made us divine –
Castor and Pollux,
Twin brothers to Helen.

We protect Theonoe,
Blessed by the gods.
She has not wronged you –
Curb your anger.

Helen goes home.
Her marriage bed waits –
She's done her duty,
Her father is pleased.

We guide her ship,
Her brothers her saviours.
Know, our dear sister –
You'll die deified.

Zeus ordains it,
Your troubles cease –
The Isle of the Blessed
Waits for Menelaus.

He has suffered more
Than humankind can bear
Since you were stolen –
Great goddess Helen.

Receive sacrifice
From moral men –
The gift of the gods
At the end of your days.

Theoclymenes

Sons of Leda and Zeus, beautiful boys,
If the gods will it, let Helen go home.
My quarrel's ended with her and my sister.
Things are settled – rest assured – no bloodshed.
Helen is loyal, most loyal of ladies.
Not many of her sex can boast the same.

All exit except the Chorus.

Chorus

    Nothing is ever as we imagine.
    The gods have their way of sorting things out.
    We must believe in what they let happen.
    We who are slaves and will be slave for ever.
    So this story ends, as do all stories.